D0844549

Amazing Amphibians

Amazing Amphibians

Sara Swan Miller

Franklin Watts
A Division of Grolier Publishing
New York • London • Hong Kong • Sydney
Danbury, Connecticut

Note to readers: Definitions for words in **bold** can be found in the Glossary at the back of this book.

Photographs ©: Animals Animals: 43 (M. Linley/OSF), 17 (Zig Leszczynski); Corbis-Bettmann/Michael & Patricia Fogden: 14, 39; ENP Images/Michael Durham: 20, 21; Heather Angel Photo Library: 5 bottom, 45; Michael & Patricia Fogden: 2, 34, 35, 38, 41, 42; NHPA: 30, 47 (A.N.T.), 10 bottom (Daniel Heuclin); Photo Researchers: 22 (Ken M. Highfill), 6 (Renee Lynn), 10 top, 16 (Tom McHugh), 25 (National Audubon Society), 36, 37 (David M. Schleser/Nature's Images Inc.), 9 (Dan Suzio), 32 (K.H. Switak); Tom Stack & Associates/Joe McDonald: 5 top, 12, 19; Visuals Unlimited: cover (Ken Lucas), 26 (Jim Merli), 28 (David Royce), 50 (G.L. Twiest).

The photograph on the cover shows a blue poison dart frog. The photograph opposite the title page shows two colorful poison dart frogs from Venezuela.

Visit Franklin Watts on the Internet at:
http://publishing.grolier.com

Library of Congress Cataloging-in-Publication Data

Miller, Sara Swan
Amazing Amphibians / by Sara Swan Miller
p. cm.— (Watts Library)
Includes bibliographical references and index.
Summary: Portrays several amphibian species with unusual appearances, habitats, or behaviors, including caecilians, tomato frogs, and midwife toads.
ISBN 0-531-11793-6 (lib. bdg.) 0-531-13980-8 (pbk.)
1. Amphibians—Juvenile literature. [1. Amphibians.] I. Title. II. Series.
QL644.2.M52 2000
597.8—dc21 99-057309

Printed in the United States of America.
1 2 3 4 5 6 7 8 9 10 R 10 09 08 07 06 05 04 03 02 01

Contents

Bullfrogs look the way frogs are "supposed" to look.

Chapter One

What Is an Amphibian?

Do you know what an amphibian is? Frogs, toads, and salamanders are amphibians—but snakes, lizards, and fish are not. So what's the difference? Scientists organize living things into categories according to specific differences and similarities. If you've learned about amphibians in school, you may know some of the ways that they are different from animals in some of the other groups, or **classes**.

Everything in Its Place

All living things can be organized into categories depending on their characteristics. Plants and animals are in two of the highest categories called **kingdoms**. Those top-level categories are broken up into many subcategories, each group having more in common than the one before. Amphibians make up one class of living things, a middle level category. Other animal classes are insects, reptiles, mammals, and birds. The science of organizing living things into such categories is called **taxonomy**.

Even if you haven't studied amphibians, you might know that amphibians are animals that spend part of their lives in the water and part on land. In fact, the word amphibian means "leading a double life." People sometimes use the word "amphibious" to describe equipment, vehicles, or machinery that can be used both on land and in the water. Most amphibians, though, start life in freshwater, then move onto the land.

Amphibians are **cold-blooded** animals with moist skins and no scales. That means an amphibian's body temperature stays about the same as the temperature of its surroundings. They need to warm up in the sun, and cool off in the shade. Amphibians are **vertebrates**—animals that have backbones. Because amphibians don't have scales to help hold in moisture, most live in damp places near the water. As long as an amphibian's skin stays moist, it can absorb oxygen through its skin. Amphibians also have lungs, just like you.

Most amphibians reproduce by laying jelly-covered eggs that have no shell. These delicate eggs must be kept moist in

A red-legged frog has laid its eggs in this pond.

Big and Small

Amphibians come in all shapes and sizes. The smallest salamander is the pigmy or dwarf Mexican salamander—it's about as big as your fingertip. The biggest salamander is the Chinese giant salamander (above), which grows to nearly 6 feet (1.8 meters) long.

The Brazilian brachycephalid frog is the smallest amphibian of all. The adult frog is smaller than your thumbnail. The goliath frog of Africa (below) measures 30 inches (75 centimeters) long with its legs stretched out. That's one big frog!

order to survive, so most amphibian females lay their eggs in water. The young that hatch from those eggs live in the water and breathe with gills. Gradually, they grow lungs and lose their gills. When they have turned into adults with lungs, they climb onto the land and live there until it is time to mate and lay their own eggs.

These are the "rules" that separate amphibians from other classes of animals. There's just one problem—amphibians don't always follow those rules! The amphibian world includes many strange animals that don't look the way we expect them to look or act the way we expect them to act. Let's get to know some of these odd amphibians.

A bullfrog waits for a fly to come by.

Chapter Two

Strange Shapes and Colors

When you hear the word *amphibian*, what kind of picture comes to mind? Do you imagine marshy ground, or little creatures swimming in a brook? Maybe, when you think of an amphibian, you see a salamander. Or maybe you picture a bullfrog or a toad. The animal in your mental picture is probably colored green or brown.

Some amphibians, though, don't seem to have the "right" number of legs or the "right" shape or color. In fact, one kind of amphibian—the caecilian (sih-SIL-yun)— probably doesn't match your mental image of amphibians at all.

Those Crazy Caecilians

A caecilian may be the strangest-looking amphibian in the world. If you saw one, you might think it was a giant worm. It's long and slimy with wormlike bands around its body. Caecilians have no legs, and their tiny eyes are covered with skin or bone. Most of them spend their entire life deep underground.

How can this wormlike caecilian be an amphibian?

The caecilian is well suited to its underground life. With its thick skull and pointed snout, it can ram its way through damp soil, as deep as 4 feet (1.2 m) down. In muddy soil, it simply wriggles its way through the earth.

Unique sensory organs called **tentacles** on each side of its snout help the caecilian find its way in the dark. With those tentacles, it can locate earthworms and other small creatures to eat.

Caecilians are odd in several ways. While other vertebrates have one set of muscles for closing their jaws, caecilians have three. Many caecilians, such as the yellow striped caecilian, have fish-like scales on their bodies.

Some caecilians actually live in the water. They swim like eels, twisting and turning through the water by bending their bodies. They can even tie themselves in knots. Sometimes they wind themselves around underwater sticks or slow-moving fish. Some people keep caecilians as aquarium pets. They call them "rubber eels," even though they aren't eels, at all, but amphibians.

Plenty of Caecilians

About 160 species of caecelians are found in tropics around the world

Strange Sirens

Most salamanders have four legs and a tail, but not the siren. The siren's front legs are tiny, and it has no back legs at all. It looks and acts more like an eel than a salamander. It spends most of its life in the water. You might see one swimming gracefully through a pond or swamp in the southeastern United States.

A greater siren is an odd salamander.

The siren is named after mythical mermaids who were said to sing beautiful songs to lure sailors to their deaths. These salamanders aren't particularly beautiful, and they certainly don't sing. The best they can do is make a small squeaking or yelping sound.

Sirens are strange in other ways too. They have tiny eyes and no eyelids. While most amphibians lose their gills and develop air-breathing lungs after they mature, sirens don't. They never lose their gills, even as adults. They need them to breathe in the water where they spend most of their time. A siren only comes out of the water and slithers through the wet grass on rainy nights.

If a siren's pond dries up, it burrows down into the mud. There it curls up in a cocoon of soapy slime with just the tip of its snout sticking out. It can live inside its cocoon for weeks or even months, waiting for the rains to come again.

Do Mudpuppies Bark?

A few other salamanders keep their gills as adults. One example is the mudpuppy. People used to say these salamanders bark like d[illegible], but actually t[illegible] are completely sil[illegible]

Congo Eels

"Congo eel" is another name for the two-toed amphiuma. This is a confusing name—it doesn't come from the Congo, and it certainly isn't an eel.

It looks a lot more like an eel than most salamanders, though. It has tiny legs that can be hard to spot, and it wriggles

Why is this two-toed amphiuma called a "Congo eel?"

through the water. Like an eel, it has gills inside its head—other salamander **larvae** have their gills on the outside of their bodies. The Congo eel has neither eyelids nor tongue—again, more like an eel than a salamander.

Congo eels spend their nights swimming in swamps in the southeastern United States. They are hunting for crayfish, frogs, small snakes, and fish. During the day, they burrow into the bottom mud. The only time they might come out on land is after a good rain. Then they can slither through the wet grass as if they were swimming.

Hairy Helpers

Amphiumas have hair cells on their body. These strange salamanders use them to sense which way the water current is flowing.

Amphibians don't usually like acidic water or soil. Congo eels, though, are different. They thrive in the acid waters of old swamps, bayous, and drainage ditches. They have adapted to make a home for themselves in difficult conditions.

Most salamanders are known to be gentle creatures, but don't ever pick up a congo eel. It can give you a nasty bite with its sharp little teeth.

The Hellbender

Many salamanders are smooth, slim, and sleek, but not the hellbender. It has a large, flattened head and wrinkled, baggy, slimy skin. It looks as though it's wearing clothes that are several sizes too large.

On land, a hellbender would look like a flat blob of jelly, but since it lives in the water, you're not likely to find one in that condition. It spends its whole life in the waters of mountain streams in the eastern United States. During the day it

This hellbender's skin looks several sizes too big.

hides under rocks in streambeds. At night, it swims out to hunt for crayfish, worms, and other small creatures.

A hellbender can't survive in **stagnant** water. It needs fast-moving streams and rivers that have plenty of oxygen mixed in with the water. Even though it has both gill slits and lungs, this salamander breathes mostly through its wrinkly skin. Wrinkled skin has more skin surface area to absorb oxygen from the water. As bizarre as it may look to you, the hellbender is well adapted to its watery world.

A Giant Relative

Hellbenders are closely related to the Chinese giant salamanders, the biggest salamanders in the world.

Hellbenders have a bad reputation. People used to say that these salamanders purposely smeared fishing lines with slime and drove the fish away. When fishers caught one by mistake, they would cut the line so that they wouldn't have to handle the slimy creature. They thought it would give them a fierce, venomous bite. Actually, although hellbenders may look scary, they are harmless creatures.

Weird Colors

What color should a frog be? You might think that all frogs are green or brown. Most frogs blend with their surroundings and escape the notice of **predators**—but some frogs use a different strategy for protection. The poison frogs of Central and South America come in brilliant colors. Some are bright blue, yellow, or black. The strawberry poison dart frog is bright red with blue legs. The orange and black poison frog is black with flashy orange patches. The dart arrow frog is bright blue.

Those colors are like a warning sign to predators, warning them to stay away. People once used the poisons in these frogs' skins to coat the tips of their blow gun darts. A species of poison frog called *Phyllobates terribilis* is so toxic that the poison in one frog's skin could kill more than 20,000 laboratory mice.

The tomato frog is another oddly colored frog. It is a bright tomato red, and it's shaped like a tomato too. We don't have to guess how this frog got its name!

A blue poison dart frog shows off its warning colors.

A cave salamander has no lungs.

Chapter Three

Bizarre Breathing

You may have learned in school that amphibians breathe with gills when they're young and develop lungs when they become adults. That's *mostly* true. Though frogs and toads do have gills as tadpoles and lungs as adults, their lungs don't work too well. Adult frogs and toads actually get most of their oxygen through the lining of their mouth and throat. They rarely fill up their lungs with air.

On the Decline

Sadly, many of the lungless salamanders and other amphibians are becoming rare and may become extinct. Their decreasing populations may be partly due to acid rain.

Of course, when it comes to amphibians, there's an exception to every rule—you already learned about a few salamanders that keep their gills after they grow up. Some other salamanders, called the lungless salamanders, never grow lungs after they lose their gills. While not being able to take in a deep breath of air might sound uncomfortable, the lungless salamanders have developed ways to cope.

Cave Salamanders

Like other lungless salamanders, cave salamanders have neither gills nor lungs as adults. They can still get enough oxygen to survive, though, as long as their skin stays moist. A lungless salamander has thin skin with plenty of blood vessels near the surface. When its skin is moist, a cave salamander can absorb oxygen directly from the air. It gets more air by absorbing oxygen through the wet lining of its mouth. If its skin dries out, though, the cave salamander will quickly suffocate.

The pretty yellow or orange cave salamanders live in limestone caves in the southeast United States, but you won't find them in other caves. When acidic water flows over limestone, a chemical reaction **neutralizes** the acid in the water. Few salamanders enjoy acid water or soil, but cave salamanders can't tolerate acidity at all. Limestone caves give these salamanders the acid-free environment they need to survive.

Because cave salamanders are so sensitive to acid, they have developed a way to sense whether water is acidic or not. Like other lungless salamanders, cave salamanders have a groove

This cave salamander is safe from acid water in its limestone cave.

running from the nose down to the upper lip. Special glands lining this groove can sense when the water is acidic and help the cave salamander find the best places to live. The groove has other uses, too. During mating season, male cave salamanders use their grooves to find females.

A newly hatched cave salamander larva would only cover half the width of a dime. It takes them a whole year to grow to 2 inches (5 cm) long because the water where the larvae live is

Handle With Care

If you ever get the chance to pick up a lungless salamander, you should wet your hands first—your warm, dry hands could kill it.

very cold, and there isn't much to eat. Finally, they lose their gills and crawl out of the water to find better feeding grounds.

If you are ever in a limestone cave, look up. You may see cave salamanders clambering about on the cave walls, hunting for insects. They tend to live near the cave entrance, where the air is moist and the light is dim. They can be very acrobatic. Sometimes they even hang from their tails like monkeys.

Slimy Salamanders

Although slimy salamanders have no lungs, they spend most of their lives on land. If you live in the eastern United States, you might find them hiding in a pile of wet leaves or in a damp log. Like cave salamanders, slimy salamanders breathe through

Never pick up a slimy salamander!

their thin skin and through the lining of their mouth and throat. Like other lungless salamanders, they have to stay moist to breathe.

Don't even think of picking up a slimy salamander. When it's scared, it produces a sticky slime all over its body that is almost impossible to wash off. This defense mechanism protects it against attacks from birds and other hungry predators. A predator that gets a mouthful of slimy salamander glue looks for other food next time.

Slimy salamanders are hard to spot. Their glossy black skin is speckled with white spots, which makes them look like fungus-covered sticks. So the next time you see something that looks like a stick covered with fungus, it may be a slimy salamander. Look twice—but remember, don't touch!

A Big Family

About 270 species of lungless salamanders live in North and South America.

Most amphibians live in or near water.

Chapter Four

Unusual Homes

If you want to find an amphibian, you probably know where to start looking. If you want to see frog tadpoles or salamander larvae, look in ponds and streams. The best place to find adult salamanders is in wet or damp places, including streams, ponds, rivers, and the damp forest floor. You might look around the banks of ponds and streams for frogs and toads, or in the damp soil of a garden. Some amphibians, though, live where you would never expect to find them.

Water-Holding Frogs

Do you think an amphibian could live in the desert? The water-holding frog does. It actually thrives in the deserts of southern Australia. If other kinds of frogs tried to live there, they'd quickly die, but the water-holding frog has developed a way to avoid drying out.

For most of the year, the desert is too hot and dry for any amphibian to survive out in the blazing sun. During this long dry season, the water-holding frog burrows down backward in the ground and waits out the heat. As it digs into its burrow,

This water-holding frog is swollen with water.

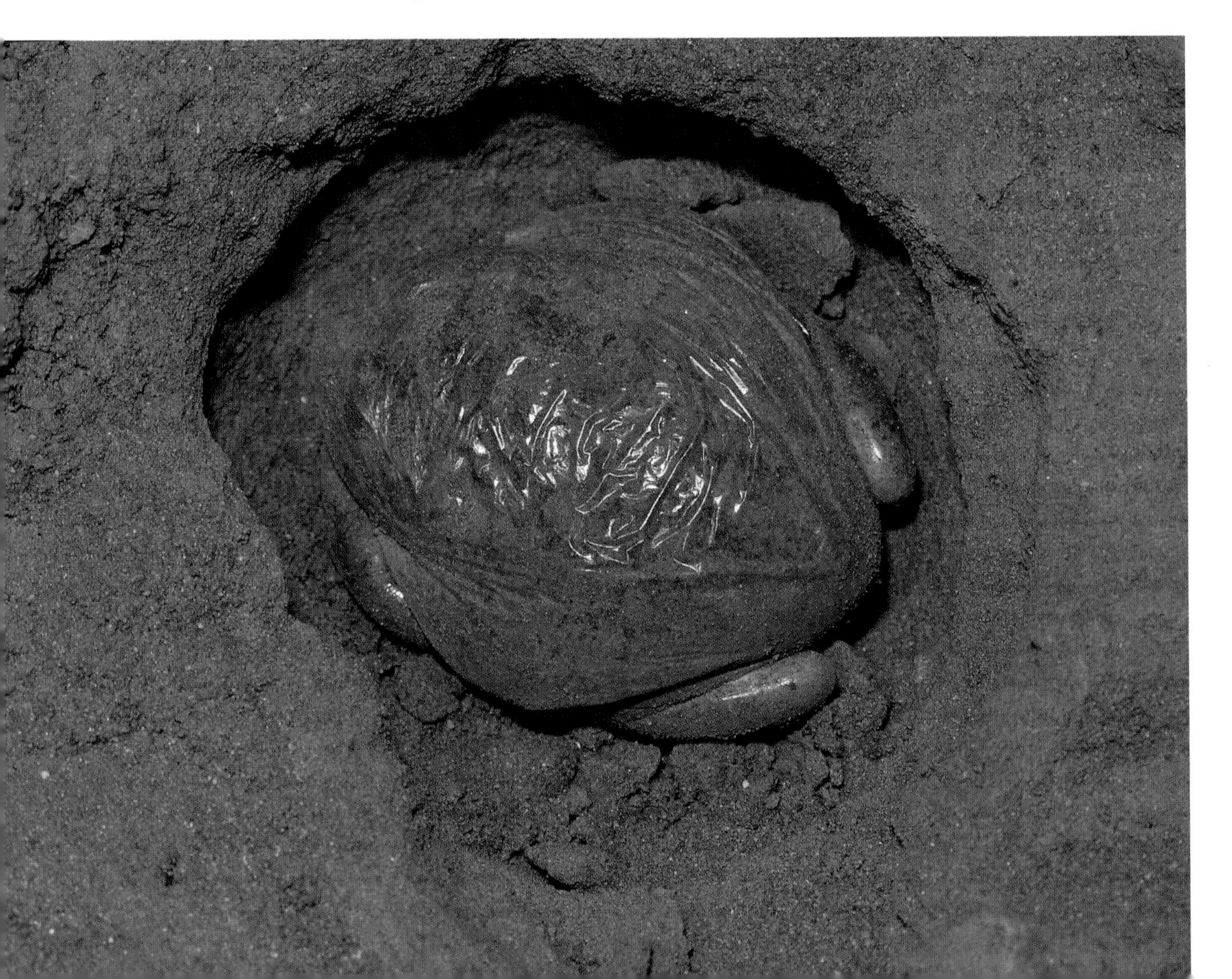

the frog sheds its skin. Its new skin secretes a slimy **mucus**. Over time, its skin and the mucus grow hard, creating a shell-like cocoon that keeps the frog from drying out. The frog also stores extra water in its bladder, which helps keep it alive. The frog's breathing and heartbeat slow way down, and it sinks into a sluggish, drowsy state.

The frog stays below the desert floor for most of the year. Finally, when the rains come, the frog tears open its cocoon and digs its way out. All of the frogs come above ground at the same time. The males and females mate, and the females lay their eggs in a shallow pool. The water in a desert pool would be too warm for any other kind of tadpole. Luckily, the tadpoles of the water-holding frog can stand high temperatures.

The pools dry up quickly, so the tadpoles don't have much time to mature. After only a few short weeks on land, they will dig themselves into the ground to wait for the next rainy season.

The frogs are safe from the heat in their burrows, but they aren't always safe from predators. Thirsty animals dig them up and eat them for the water they hold. Sometimes, even people search them out and squeeze the water from their bladders. Any water is welcome in the dry desert.

Arboreal Salamanders

Would you look for a salamander high up in a tree? Not usually, but that's where you would find the arboreal salamander. It is the champion climber of the salamander world. One

An arboreal salamander clings to a tree trunk.

arboreal salamander was once found in a red tree mouse's nest—60 feet (18.3 m) high in a tree.

Arboreal salamanders have become adapted to climbing about in trees, hunting for insects. They have large toe pads that help them stick to tree trunks and a grasping tail that helps them cling to branches. They live mainly along the coast of California. If you see one, you may soon see many more, because arboreal salamanders like to cluster in groups. You might find thirty or so packed together in one tree hole. Sometimes they come down to the ground to hunt for insects. There, they may hide in stumps or rock walls, or even underground in basements.

Arboreal salamanders are odd in other ways too. Most salamanders have tiny, spiny teeth, but arboreal salamanders have large knife-like teeth in their lower jaws. Scientists think they may use those large teeth to scrape fungus out of tree holes. If that's true, they are the only salamanders that eat fungus. Another odd thing about these lungless salamanders is that they can breathe through their toes as well as through their skin and mouth lining.

Most salamanders are silent—they have no vocal cords to make sounds with. When an arboreal salamander is scared, though, it makes a squeaking sound. The salamander forces air through its jaws and nostrils with its throat muscles. It's amazing that an animal with no lungs or vocal cords can make any sound at all. It sounds like a mouse—but it's a salamander!

Malayan Flying Frogs

Many species of tree frogs have sticky adhesive pads on their toes. The pads help the frogs cling to tree trunks and branches. Believe it or not a few kinds of tree frogs can fly through the air!

The Malayan flying frog of Southeast Asia doesn't actually flap its wings and fly, but it parachutes from tree to tree. Its extra-long fingers and toes have webbing between them. To glide from one tree to another, it spreads out its fingers and toes and jumps. Its huge webbed feet slow its fall and act like rudders to help it steer. A flying frog can parachute down as far as 100 feet (30 m) and land with a plop on the trunk of another tree.

When they're not in the air, flying frogs usually climb about in the trees, hunting for insects to gobble up. Their sticky toe pads allow them to walk straight up or down a tree trunk. A flying frog can even walk up a pane of glass. Those are very special toes!

More "Flying" Frogs

Three other web-toed frogs are known to parachute from tree to tree. These are all the ones we know about—there may be even more.

A red-eyed gliding leaf frog takes to the air.

A string of eggs laid by a Gulf Coast frog.

Chapter Five

Odd Egg-laying

Have you ever seen a glob or string of squishy-looking jelly in a pond? You were probably looking at a mass of eggs laid by an amphibian. Amphibian eggs have no shells to protect them, so adult amphibians usually lay their eggs in water to keep them wet. Then the parents swim away, leaving the eggs to hatch on their own. Of course, it would be wrong to say that all amphibians lay eggs in the water, that all amphibians lay their eggs and swim away, or even that all amphibians even lay eggs. By now, you've probably realized that many amphibians break the "rules."

Foam Nest Tree Frogs

You've already learned about the arboreal salamanders, and some frogs that spend most of their time in the trees. It might be harder to believe, though, that some frogs lay their eggs high up in the trees. Over millions of years the African gray tree frogs have **evolved** a wonderful way to protect their eggs and keep them from drying out—they make a nest of water-holding foam in the trees.

These African gray tree frogs are making a foam nest.

These tree frogs usually live inland, but in the spring they all head for trees overhanging a pond. Several of them gather

together on a branch. The females start laying their eggs along with a lot of liquid. Then all the frogs use their webbed back legs to stir the liquid into a froth, like beating egg whites with an eggbeater. They keep beating until all the females have laid their eggs, and they have created a big foam nest. It may take up to three hours.

Soon the foam nest dries on the outside and turns crusty and brown. That makes the eggs inside safe from many preda-

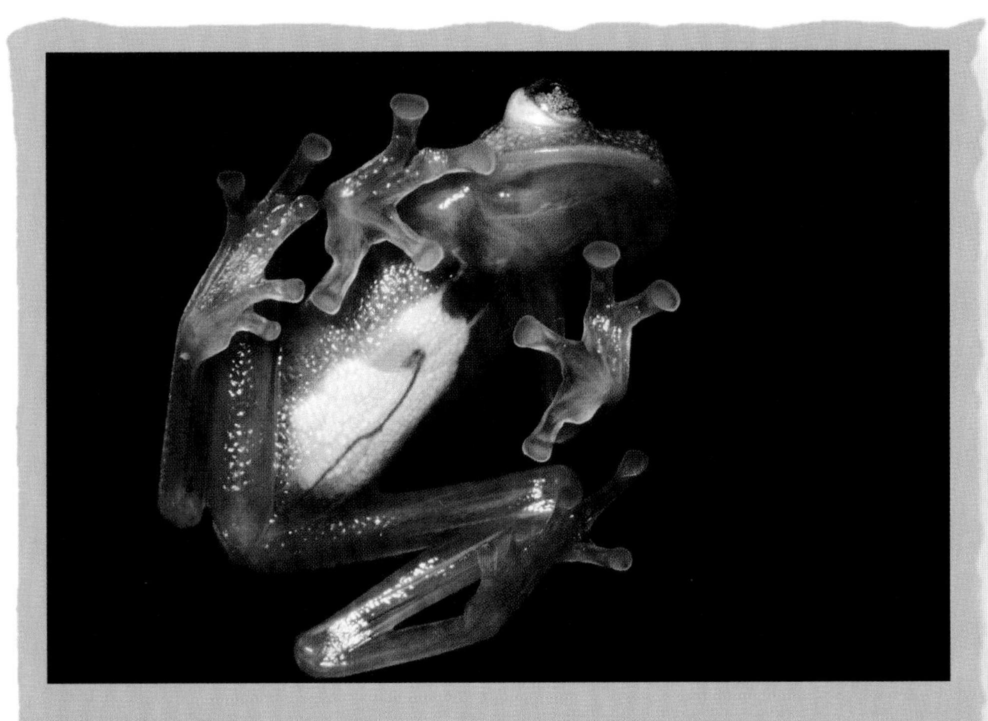

Glass Frogs

The glass frogs of Central and South America lay their eggs in trees, but they don't make nests. Their eggs stick to the leaves. The males stay nearby to guard them and protect them from predators. These frogs are called glass frogs because you can see through the skin on their bellies and watch their hearts beat!

tors, and the wet foam around the eggs keeps them from drying out. The females stay at the nest and keep it just wet enough. A few days later, the tadpoles hatch. They swim about inside the nest for a few days. The warmth they generate as they swim gradually melts the nest. Then the tadpoles fall into the water below.

Once they become adults, the young frogs climb into the trees. Like other tree frogs, they have sticky pads on their toes that help them cling to tree trunks and branches. Their fingers and toes are adapted for life in the trees in another way too. The two inner toes are opposable to the two outer toes, much as your thumb is opposable to your other fingers. This special arrangement helps tree frogs hold tightly to twigs.

Darwin's Frogs

The famous naturalist Charles Darwin discovered these frogs on a trip to South America. The male Darwin's frog has a very strange way of taking care of the young. The female lays her eggs on the damp ground, and the male sits nearby and watches. Finally, when he sees the tadpoles wiggling about inside the eggs, he snaps them up in his mouth—but he's not looking for a quick meal. He stores the eggs to keep them.

Not the Only One

The male of a related species, *Rhinoderma rufum,* also scoops the eggs up in his mouth. Then he carries them down to the water.

The male has long vocal sacs running down each side of his body. During the mating season, he uses those vocal sacs to make calls to attract a mate. During breeding time, though, they make a perfect place to protect the young tadpoles from predators.

Young Darwin's frogs have just leaped from their father's mouth.

There's nothing to eat in the vocal sacs, but the tadpoles can live off **yolk sacs**, bags of nutrients inside their eggs, as they develop. After two or three months, the tadpoles are ready for life on their own. Their father opens his mouth, and a dozen tiny frogs come hopping out!

Marsupial Frogs

When you hear the word marsupial, you probably think of a kangaroo with a baby sticking its head out of her pouch. Most marsupials have a pouch where their babies grow. If you know that, and you know that there's a kind of frog that carries its eggs in a pouch, it's not too hard to guess how the marsupial frog got its name.

This female pygmy marsupial frog has a pouchful of eggs.

A female marsupial frog's pouch is on her back, however, not on her belly. After mating, the male stays nearby until the female begins laying her eggs. Using his front feet, he pushes the eggs into her pouch.

The female can carry as many as 100 eggs in her "backpack." Just before they hatch, the female looks extremely swollen and lumpy. Because the skin of the pouch is very thin, you can actually see the eggs inside.

When the eggs are ready to hatch, the female slips into the water. Using her back toes, she pulls apart the slit-like opening of her pouch, and the tadpoles swim away. Now the fragile tadpoles have to fend for themselves.

Midwife Toads

A midwife toad is another amphibian that takes care of its young in an unusual way. She lets the male carry and protect her load of eggs.

These small toads live in Europe and northern Africa. In the spring, the woods echo with the owl-like sounds of males calling to females. Once they find a partner, they mate on the ground, instead of in the water like most amphibians. A male clasps a female from behind as she lays a double string of eggs. He wraps the eggs around his hind legs, and the female hops away. Then the male goes off to find a damp place where he can protect the eggs.

Eggs on Her Back

A related frog doesn't have a pouch, but she still carries her eggs about on her back. The sticky eggs cling on their own.

A male midwife toad carts his eggs around on his back legs.

For several weeks, the male carries this load of young wherever he goes. During the day, he hides under logs and stones. At night, when he hops out to hunt for insects, the eggs stay moist in the dew. Sometimes, in dry weather, he jumps into a pond to moisten the eggs.

Finally, when the eggs are ready to hatch, the male travels to a pond and puts the tadpoles into the water. The tadpoles are defenseless on their own, and grow very slowly. With so many hungry fish and large predatory insects out hunting them, few tadpoles survive their first year.

Those that reach adulthood and leave the pond, however, are usually safe. The adults have warts on their backs that contain a very strong poison, so most predators leave them alone.

Hop on Pop

A male Australian midwife toad also takes care of the young. The newly hatched tadpoles wriggle into pouches on his sides.

Surinam Toads

The Surinam toad of eastern and northern South America may be one of the world's weirdest toads. It has an oddly flattened body, a big, flat triangular head with tiny eyes, and two tubelike nostrils sticking out of its snout. Its front legs are very short and delicate.

A Surinam toad has no tongue, but it uses its sensitive star-shaped pads on their fingertips to probe for food on the muddy river bottom. It stuffs its food into its mouth with its front feet. The Surinam toad has no vocal cords—but the male has bony rods inside his throat that he uses to make a clicking, ticking sound to call to his mate.

A female Surinam toad carries newly laid eggs.

Perhaps the most unusual thing about these strange toads is the way they reproduce. While in the water, a male clasps a female from behind with his front legs wrapped around her back legs. The two then rise to the surface, and flip over to float on their backs. Then the female lays an egg that falls onto the male's belly. They flip over again, and the male lets the egg fall onto the female's back, where he fertilizes it. The toads do these flips over and over, until sixty or more eggs are sticking to the female's back. Oddly, the eggs stick to the female's back, but not to the male's belly or to each other.

Gradually, the eggs sink into their mother's back. Skin grows over them until they are encased in pits with horny lids. The mother carries the developing young around with her wherever she goes. The tadpoles use their tails to help them absorb extra oxygen while they are embedded in her back.

Finally, after three to five months, the little toads pop out. They look just like their mother, but they are only 1 inch (2.5 cm) long.

Gastric Brooding Frogs

Australia is full of strange animals, including odd amphibians. One of the most unusual Australian amphibians, the gastric brooding frog, is now thought to be extinct—but when it existed it was one of the strangest frogs around. Gastric brooding frog young actually developed inside eggs in the stomach of their mother. After the male and female gastric brooding frog mated, the female swallowed the fertilized eggs.

Another Solution

Tadpoles of a related species, *Rheobatrachus vitellinus*, also develop in their mother's stomach. However, they don't create chemicals that shut down their mother's digestion. Instead, the tadpoles are protected from her digestive fluids by a layer of mucus.

A special protective jelly around the eggs, as well as certain chemicals the tadpoles produced, shut down the mother's digestive juices and kept the eggs from being dissolved in her stomach.

Perhaps those chemicals shut down her appetite, too—for 6 long weeks, the female gastric brooding frog did not eat. Finally, froglets came hopping out of her mouth, and her life returned to normal.

For centuries, people thought that there were no aquatic frogs in Australia. Then, in 1972, the gastric brooding frog was discovered. This small, timid frog spent most of its time hiding under stones on streambeds.

No one has seen the gastric brooding frog in the wild for many years. Scientists were hoping to learn more about how the eggs and tadpoles shut down their mother's digestive juices in order to help people with stomach ulcers. Unfortunately, these fascinating frogs may never be seen again.

Mount Nimba Toads

The female Mount Nimba toad lives in Africa and never lays eggs. This toad carries her young inside her body like a mammal and gives birth to live young. She carries her developing young inside her body until they are born as fully formed toads.

After the female mates, the young grow inside her body in a tube called an **oviduct** (OH-vih-dukt), which usually carries eggs out of the body. In a Mount Nimba toad, though, the young develop in the oviduct. Unlike mammal embryos, the toad larvae have no **placenta** to nourish them and give them oxygen. The wall of the mother's oviduct is full of blood vessels that supply the young with oxygen and nourishment. However, as many as a hundred larvae may be in the oviduct, and each individual larva can't always be next to the nutrient-carrying wall. If you could look inside, you would see that the larvae have very long, slender tails. Those tails aren't for

Three Ways to Bear Young

Most insects, fish, amphibians, reptiles, and all birds lay eggs that hatch outside of the mother's body. The eggs of some animals hatch inside the mother's body and are born live. The young of other animals, including most mammals, aren't protected by an egg. Instead, they are nurtured inside their mother. They live off nutrients from her body until they are born.

swimming. Away from the oviduct wall, a larva can still get nourishment and oxygen through its long tail. So each larva has a decent chance of survival, even in the crowded oviduct.

The Mount Nimba toad is the only live-bearing toad in the world. You could never tell by looking at this toad that it's so unusual, however. It looks like any other squat, short-legged, warty toad.

Chapter Six

Those Amazing Amphibians

The amphibian world has so many exceptions to the "rules" that you might start wondering where the rules came from in the first place. In this book, you've learned about amphibians that probably don't match your mental picture of what amphibians look like, about frogs, toads, and salamanders that live in unusual places, and about amphibians that reproduce in strange ways. All these odd amphibians have developed special ways to survive in their habitats.

Now that you have learned about some of the amphibians that break the rules, you may have a different idea of what an amphibian really is. The next time someone asks you what an amphibian is, you might have some new answers. You might say that "*Most* amphibians lay their eggs in the water," or "*Most* amphibians live in water as tadpoles and on land as adults." You'd be right to say that "*Most* adult amphibians breathe with lungs and live in moist places," and that "*Most* amphibians have four legs." Then you could go on to describe some of the really strange amphibians that break all the rules. Amphibians certainly are amazing!

Opposite: A spotted salamander rests on a log.

Amazing Amphibians Around the World

Common name	Scientific name	Where found
Pygmy salamander, dwarf Mexican salamander	*Thorius* spp.	Mexico
Giant salamander	*Andrias dividianus*	Western China
Brachycephalid frogs	*Brachycephalus* sp.	Southeastern South America
Goliath frog	*Conraua goliath*	Western Africa
Caecilians	*Gymnophiona* sp.	Tropical and warm temperate regions in South America, southern Asia, and parts of Africa
Sirens	family *Sirenidae*	Swamps in southeastern USA
Congo eel, two-toed amphiuma	*Amphiuma means*	Southeastern USA—Louisiana to Virginia
Hellbender	*Cryptobranchus alleganinesis*	Drainage areas of the Susquehanna, Ohio, Missouri and Mississippi rivers
Strawberry poison dart frog	*Dendrobates pumilio*	Nicaragua to the Amazon, Bolivia, the Guianas, and southeastern Brazil
Orange and black poison frog	*Dendrobates leucomelas*	Nicaragua to the Amazon, Bolivia, the Guianas, and southeastern Brazil
Dart arrow frog	*Dendrobates azureus*	Southern part of Surinam
Tomato frog	*Dyscophus antogilii*	Lowlands of Madagascar
Cave salamander	*Eurycea lucifuga*	In and around caves in southeastern and central USA
Slimy salamander	*Plethodon glutinosus*	Eastern USA

Water-holding frog	*Cyclorana platycephala*	Deserts of southern Australia
Arboreal salamander	*Aneides lugubris*	Along the California coastline and a small part of northwestern Mexico
Malayan flying frog	*Rhacophorus reinwardtii*	Southeast Asia
Foam nest tree frog	*Chiromantis xerampelina*	Africa
Glass frogs	family *Centrolenidae*	Mexico, Central and South America
Darwin's frog	*Rhinoderma darwinii*	Mostly Argentina and Chile
Marsupial frogs	*Gastrotheca* sp.	Tropical South America
Midwife toad	*Alytes obstetricans* and *A. cisternasii*	Western Europe
Surinam toad	*Pipa pipa*	Eastern and northern South America
Gastric brooding frog	*Rheobatrachus silus*	Extinct, once found in Australia
Mount Nimba toad	*Nectophrynoides occidentalis*	In Africa around Mt. Nimba, including parts of Guinea, Côte d'Ivoire, and Liberia

Glossary

class—a group of creatures that share certain characteristics. Caecilians, salamanders, and frogs and toads are all in the same class—the amphibians.

cold-blooded—an animal whose body temperature depends on the environment

evolve—to change slowly over generations, developing specialized physical characteristics or behaviors

kingdom—the top-level category for classifying living things. The five kingdoms are fungi, plants, animals, protists, and bacteria.

larva—(plural larvae) an immature stage of an animal life cycle

mucus—a slimy substance produced by an animal, often as a protective coating

neutralize—to make harmless

oviduct—a tube leading from the ovaries through which a female's eggs are passed out

placenta—a structure with many blood vessels in the uterus of most mammals that nourishes the embryo

predator—an animal that hunts another animal

stagnant—still or very slow-moving water

taxonomy—the science of organizing living things into categories

tentacles—sensory organs of some animals, including caecilians

vertebrate—an animal that has a backbone

yolk sacs—bags of nutrients inside an egg

To Find Out More

Books

Badger, David P. *Frogs*. New York: Voyageur Press, 2000.

Clarke, Dr. Barry. *Amphibian*. New York: Alfred A. Knopf, 1993.

Gerholdt, James E. *Salamanders*. Minneapolis, MN: Abdo and Daughters, 1994.

Julivert, Maria Angels. *The Fascinating World of Frogs and Toads*. Hauppage, NY: Barrons Juveniles, 1993.

Lovett, Sarah. *Extremely Weird Frogs*. Santa Fe, NM: John Muir Publications, 1996.

Martin, James. *Frogs*. New York: Crown, 1997.

Maruska, Edward J. *Amphibians: Creatures of Land and Water.* Danbury, CT: Franklin Watts, 1994.

Ricciuti, Edward. *Amphibians.* Woodbridge, CT: Blackbirch, 1994.

Snedden, Robert. *What Is an Amphibian?* San Francisco: Sierra Club Juveniles, 1994.

Stotsky, Sandra. *Let's Hear it for Herps! All About Reptiles and Amphibians*. Broomall, PA: Chelsea House, 1998.

Organizations and Online Sites

Exploratorium: Frogs
http://www.exploratorium.edu/frogs/
This online exhibit includes information about frog biology, biographies of scientists studying frogs, and frog sounds.

Frogwatch Ontario
http://www.cciw.ca/frogwatching/
This Canadian program is collecting information from volunteer frogwatchers about the frogs that they see or hear in their neighborhoods.

Frogwatch USA

http://www.mp2-pwrc.usgs.gov/frogwatch/index.htm

Frogwatch USA is a network of volunteers collecting information about frogs throughout the United States. You can volunteer too!

U.S. Fish and Wildlife Service

http://www.fws.gov

This United States government agency has information on endangered species, habitat conservation, and more.

The Wordwidekids Network–Reptiles and Amphibians

http://www.worldkids.com/critter/reptiles/wel/

This site offers information about these animals and a questions and answers section.

Yahooligans

http://www.yahooligans.com/Science_and_Nature/Living_Things/Reptiles_and_Amphibians/

This directory can provide links to articles and information on reptiles and amphibians.

A Note on Sources

When I began this book, I first searched my memories. Over the years I have taken numerous courses in natural history and visited dozens of zoos, aquariums, and nature preserves around the world. Thinking about those experiences gave me more ideas of strange amphibians to include. My next step was to browse through my personal nature library for ideas and facts. Palmer and Fowler's *Handbook of Natural History*, even though it is very old-fashioned and incomplete, gave me leads about various species to include. *The Encyclopedia of Reptiles & Amphibians* is an excellent reference book that provides an in-depth understanding of the various families and species. Simon and Schuster's guide to *Reptiles and Amphibians of the World* is a handy field guide with pictures and brief descriptions. I supplemented these with books from local libraries, including children's books.

Finally, once I knew which species I wanted to include, I went to the Internet. By searching for a specific genus and species, I often found useful information, particularly in sites posted by universities and zoos.

The help of expert consultant Kathy Carlstead, Ph.D., of the Honolulu Zoo in Honolulu, Hawaii, was invaluable in creating this book.

—*Sara Swan Miller*

Index

Numbers in *italics* indicate illustrations.

About the Author

Sara Swan Miller has enjoyed working with children all her life, first as a Montessori nursery-school teacher and later as an outdoor environmental educator at the Mohonk Preserve in New Paltz, New York. As director of the school program, she has taught hundreds of children the importance of appreciating and respecting the natural world.

She has written more than 30 books, including *Three Stories You Can Read to Your Dog; Three Stories You Can Read to Your Cat; Three More Stories You Can Read to Your Dog;* and *What's in the Woods? An Outdoor Activity Book*, as well as four other books on strange animals for the Watts Library. She has also written several True Books on farm animals for Children's Press, and more than a dozen books for Franklin Watts's *Animals in Order* series.